OVER IN THE MEADOW

OVER IN THE MEADOW

By Olive A. Wadsworth
Set to simple music
by Mabel Wood Hill

The pictures of all the
Meadow People were
drawn by Harold Sichel

MORGAN SHEPARD COMPANY
NEW YORK·SAN FRANCISCO·1906

You might as well keep smilin'
For there aint a bit o' sense
Of fidgetin' and ritin',
And longin' too intense,
For most things worth the getting
Are sure to find their way
Where you in peace are setting
With a smile upon your face

To little Gene.
with

This Book is
Dedicated to
RICHARDSON KING WOOD
(a little Boy)

THE MUSIC
BY MABEL WOOD HILL

Moderato

Over in the meadow In the sand, in the sun, lives an

old Mother Toad And her little Toadie one.

MOTHER TOAD

Little Toads most always are
  Happy Toads, and kind;
When their mother asks them things,
  Toadies always mind.
When they're told to go to bed,
  Or to wash their hands,
Every well-bred little Toad,
  Minds and understands.
        So do you?

THE TOADS

VER in the meadow,
   In the sand, in the sun,
Lived an old mother-toad
And her little toadie one.
"Wink!" said the mother;
   "I wink," said the one:
So she winked and she blinked
   In the sand, in the sun.

MOTHER FISH

Baby Fish are very small,
  But their mother knows
Just the place to learn to swim,
  Where the water goes.
If she tells them not to go
  On the land to play,
They don't grumble or complain;
  Baby Fish obey.
      So do you?

THE FISHES

OVER in the meadow,
　　Where the stream runs blue,
Lived an old mother-fish
　And her little fishes two.
"Swim!" said the mother;
　"We swim," said the two:
So they swam and they leaped
　Where the stream runs blue.

MOTHER BLUE-BIRD

Baby Blue-Birds are genteel,
   They don't scratch or bite.
And when Birdies talk to them
   They are real polite.
If Jim Crow <u>is</u> rough and gruff,
   That's no reason why
Blue-Birds can't be courteous,
   They at least can try.
      So can you.

THE BLUE-BIRDS

OVER in the meadow,
  In a hole in a tree,
Lived a mother-blue-bird
And her little birdies three.
"Sing!" said the mother;
  "We sing," said the three:
So they sang, and were glad,
  In the hole in the tree.

MOTHER MUSKRAT

Little Muskrats dig in mud
  With their mouths and feet,
But they always bathe a lot,
  So are clean and neat.
Never were good, little Rats
  Known to tell you lies;
They just tell the truth and look
  Straight in mother's eyes.
    So do you?

THE MUSKRATS

OVER in the meadow,
  In the reeds on the shore,
Lived a mother-muskrat
And her little ratties four.
"Dive!" said the mother;
  "We dive," said the four:
So they dived and they burrowed
  In the reeds on the shore.

MOTHER ·HONEY-BEE

Little Honey-bees are smart;
   They are funny too,
For they work like everything,
   Seldom getting through.
Work for Honey-bees is play;
   Play for them is work.
Bizzy, buzzy, happy Bees,
   Never sulk or shirk.
      Just like you.

THE HONEY·BEES

VER in the meadow,
  In a snug beehive,
  Lived a mother-honeybee
And her little honeys five.
"Buzz!" said the mother;
  "We buzz," said the five:
So they buzzed and they hummed
  In the snug beehive.

MOTHER CROW

Little Baby Blacky Crows,
  Caw when mother caws,
Never hiding mouth or eyes
  With their little claws.
They just like to go at once
  Up into their nest,
For they know that mother knows
  Just the thing that's best.
    So do you.

THE CROWS

VER in the meadow,
  In a nest built of sticks,
  Lived a black mother-crow
And her little crows six.
"Caw!" said the mother;
  "We caw," said the six:
So they cawed and they called
  In their nest built of sticks.

MOTHER CRICKET

Little Crickets chip and chirp,
  In the meadow grass;
Singing, jolly all the time
  As the hours pass.
Never do they sulk or pout,
  Moping under ground;
Folks are glad when they're about,
  Folks want them around.
    Just like you.

THE CRICKETS

OVER in the meadow,
Where the grass is so even,
Lived a gay mother-cricket
And her little crickets seven.
"Chirp!" said the mother;
"We chirp," said the seven:
So they chirped cheery notes
In the grass soft and even.

MOTHER LIZARD

Little Lizards love to play
   In the golden sun,
'Cause it's very good for them
   And because it's fun.
But when mother tells them to
   Study from their books,
Lizards never whine or cry,
   Or give sulky looks.
     Nor do you.

THE LIZARDS

VER in the meadow,
　　By the old mossy gate,
　　Lived a brown mother-lizard
And her little lizards eight.
"Bask!" said the mother;
　"We bask," said the eight:
So they basked in the sun
　On the old mossy gate.

MOTHER OWL

Little Owls like the night
  Better than the day.
They aren't frightened in the dark:
  "Dark can't hurt," they say.
And they eat exactly what's
  Given them for food;
Saying "Thank you, mother," and
  Chewing fine and good.
      So do you.

THE OWLS

OVER in the meadow,
   Near the post-road sign,
   Lives a gray mother-owl
And her little owlies nine.
"Hoot!" said the mother;
   "We hoot," said the nine:
So they hooted and they tooted
   Near the post-road sign.

MOTHER SQUIRREL

Little Squirrels chatter some;
  So do Girls and Boys;
But their jolly chattering
  Never once annoys
Mother Squirrel, for you see,
  They don't shout or shriek,
But use gentle words and voice
  Always when they speak.
    Just like you.

THE SQUIRRELS

OVER in the meadow,
  In a cozy little den,
  Lives an old mother-squirrel
And her little squirrels ten.
"Munch!" said the mother;
  "We munch," said the ten:
So they munched and they crunched
  In the cozy little den.

MOTHER LARK

Little Larks are dear as dear,
  Every song they sing
Bubbles from their throats and hearts
  Like a crystal spring.
That's because their thoughts are pure,
  And their hearts are glad.
So they never think or say
  Naughty things, or bad.
      Nor do you.

THE LARKS

OVER in the meadow,
   Where the grass touches heaven,
   Lives an old mother-lark
And her little larkies eleven.
"Soar!" said the mother;
   "We soar," said the eleven:
So they soared and they soared
   Up, up into heaven.

MOTHER DRAGON-FLY

Little Dragon-flies are smart;
   They are quick and spry,
All around they flit and go,
   But they always fly
Home again before the sun
   Drops far out of sight.
Then they're put to bed and say,
   "Mother, dear, GOOD NIGHT."
      So do you.

❋THE DRAGON-FLIES❋

 VER in the meadow,
    Where the gray rocks shelve,
Lives a mother-dragon-fly
  And her little dragons twelve.
"Hum!" said the mother;
  "We hum," said the twelve:
So they hummed in the sun
  Where the gray rocks shelve.

TO THE CHILDREN

Quite a lot of people have worked together to make this little Book for you. Perhaps you would like to know who they were.

Years ago, a Lady whose name was Olive A. Wadsworth, wrote *twelve* verses called "OVER IN THE MEADOW." The first *eight*, the Printer Man has given you; the last *four* are new verses, because a certain little boy liked to hear about baby Owls, Squirrels, Larks, and Dragon-flies, so another Lady, whose name is Marguerite Richardson Wood, wrote about the Owls, Squirrels, Larks, and Dragon-flies. The Lady hopes you will like to hear about them.

Then another Lady composed the music for you to sing. Her name is Mabel Wood Hill. Then a smart young man drew all the pictures to make this book nice. He likes Children most, and Animals and Things next. He liked to make the pictures. His name is Harold Sichel.

Then the twelve little sermons were all written by a Man who hopes you will not dislike him for preaching. He will not tell his name, for fear that some day you might meet him and run away.

Then the Book was made into a Book by a Cor-po-ra-tion, called MORGAN SHEPARD COMPANY. (Do you know what a Cor-po-ra-tion is? I do not.)

I think that is all I will say about it.

MAN.

New York, October 1st,
    1 9 0 6 .

Lightning Source UK Ltd.
Milton Keynes UK
UKHW022335060223
416579UK00001B/27